SANTA LIVES!

ELLIS WEINER

Riverhead Books
New York

SANTA LIVES!

THE BERKLEY PUBLISHING GROUP
Published by the Penguin Group
Penguin Group (USA) Inc.
375 Hudson Street, New York, New York 10014, USA
Penguin Group (Canada), 90 Eglinton Avenue East, Suite 700, Toronto, Ontario M4P 2Y3, Canada
(a division of Pearson Penguin Canada Inc.)
Penguin Books Ltd., 80 Strand, London WC2R 0RL, England
Penguin Group Ireland, 25 St. Stephen's Green, Dublin 2, Ireland (a division of Penguin Books Ltd.)
Penguin Group (Australia), 250 Camberwell Road, Camberwell, Victoria 3124, Australia
(a division of Pearson Australia Group Pty. Ltd.)
Penguin Books India Pvt. Ltd., 11 Community Centre, Panchsheel Park, New Delhi—110 017, India
Penguin Group (NZ), cnr Airborne and Rosedale Roads, Albany, Auckland 1310, New Zealand
(a division of Pearson New Zealand Ltd.)
Penguin Books (South Africa) (Pty.) Ltd., 24 Sturdee Avenue, Rosebank, Johannesburg 2196,
South Africa

Penguin Books Ltd., Registered Offices: 80 Strand, London WC2R 0RL, England

First Riverhead trade paperback edition: November 2005

Library of Congress Cataloging-in-Publication Data

Weiner, Ellis.
    Santa lives! : five conclusive arguments for the existence of Santa Claus / by Ellis Weiner.— 1st
Riverhead trade pbk. ed.
        p. cm.
    ISBN 1-59448-154-7
    1. Santa Claus. I. Title.

GT4985.W435 2005
394.2663—dc22

                                                                                    2005044332

PRINTED IN THE UNITED STATES OF AMERICA

10 9 8 7 6 5 4 3 2 1

CONTENTS

SANTA LIVES!

Santa entering chimney. Although the
moon is behind him, his face is well lit—proof
of his quasi-divinity.

Introduction

THE figure of Santa Claus is shrouded in mystery and contradiction.

Well before the founding of the Christian Church, men (and women, if the men let them go outside) would gaze up at the heavens during the bleakest, longest nights of the year and wail, although probably not in English, "Who will deliver us from this endless wintry gloom? What can sustain us through the long nights ahead besides heavy drinking, the worship of moss, and staring at endless reruns of the Bronze Age equivalent of *Law & Order?*" Then would every heart beat with a single desire and every voice give utterance to the same wish: "Isn't there some big fat man up there who can come down here and give me free stuff?"[1]

In response to such universal human longing, Santa Claus appears.

And yet, from the first, he is a figure of controversy. It begins with his very name: *Santa*, scholars tell us, is the *feminine* form of the Spanish/Italian/Portuguese word for "saint." But *Claus* is a masculine Nordic/Germanic name. Is Santa Claus a girl with a boy's name or a boy with a girl's name or what? It's worse than Leslie or Alex!

No wonder, then, that when we (henceforth, by "we" I will mean not only those of us in the intellectual elite but everyone else, too!) first think of Santa Claus, we

---

1 Early polytheistic cultures had their own proto-versions of Santa Claus, the most familiar of which comes down to us from the ancient Egyptians, as seen on the funerary offerings on the tomb of Ka aper (2465–20 B.C.; Old Kingdom, early Dynasty 5). The painted limestone bas relief depicts, among the familiar images of vessels, snakes, birds, and eyes, a portly, bearded man standing in a chariot equipped with snow runners and being drawn by a team of creatures, each featuring the head of a reindeer and the body of an elf. (History is silent on where, in ancient Egypt, there was snow. Indeed, we know of no hieroglyph for the idea, although the Egyptians did possess twenty-three different hieroglyphs for "sand.")

Among the ancients the Claus figure finds its most enduring form in that of the Roman deity Gratuitas (goddess of tips). Santa and his precursors disappear entirely with the advent of Judaic

think of a hermaphrodite. And no wonder that, when we ask ourselves where he's from, we instantly decide: Switzerland, where everyone is half Italian and half German and half French, where the boys wear dresses and learn to curtsy, where the girls smoke pipes and enjoy a good arm wrestle, and which is home to the highest percentage of Swiss hermaphrodites in the world. And yet, no matter how often we repeat to one another, "Santa Claus is a Swiss hermaphrodite," it is never fully credible, never entirely satisfying. Then we are shown the familiar figure in the red suit, and we don't know *what* to think.

But that is only the beginning of our dilemma. If he (if indeed he is a "he") is Santa Claus, how can he also

---

monotheism; it is Jehovah Himself who is the giver of gifts and to whom the traditional prayer, "Ohmigod, Thou Shouldns't Have," is directed:

> *O Lord of hosts*
> *It is perfect.*
> *It is just what I wanted.*
> *How didst Thou know?*
> *O but wait. I am as a dunce.*
> *Thou art the All One and*
> *Knowest everything.*
> *Anyway, seriously.*
> *I love it.*
> *For is this robin's egg blue not*

be, as he is alternatively called, Saint Nicholas? Or Father Christmas? Or Père Noel? And exactly where does the modern world get off calling him the vulgar, overly familiar Saint Nick? How, in any reasonable universe, can a Christian saint be named Nick? What next? Saint Chet? Saint Tiffany?

And what's with "Kris Kringle"? Isn't that a brand of doughnuts?

Still, at the end of the day—or, more accurately, of the year—we manage to reconcile ourselves to living with these and other unresolved issues. Christmas, as it always does, comes. We betake to festoon the bowers with gaudy bunting and hoist a schooner high to quaff the foaming wassail, although we haven't the faintest

---

Mine favorite of all the colors?
And behold how it fits!
For yea, it chafeth not, neither doth it itch.
Blessed art Thou
O Lord our God
King of the Universe
Who knoweth what we want
And our exact size.
Thou shouldns't have.
(Amen.)

It is finally with the rise of Christianity in the late nineteenth century that we encounter the recognizable figure of the modern Santa Claus.

idea what the hell any of that means. Then we welcome Santa Claus into our homes and our department stores, our malls and our children's hospitals, our drunken office parties and our drunken Chanukah parties and our drunken Kwanzaa parties. Or rather—and we know this all too well, no matter how strenuously we pretend to believe otherwise—we welcome not Santa Claus himself but "Santa Claus," i.e., a stand-in, a make-believe substitute for the real Claus.

Invariably this ersatz Santa—usually embodied by a classroom father, a pediatric resident, or Tyler, the numbskull in Purchasing—dispatches his duties adequately, distributing presents and frightening children, embarrassing everyone and "good-naturedly" groping teachers, nurses, and secretaries, sometimes all at once. And yet, throughout, we are haunted by a perennially unresolved question:

Is there an actual personage upon whom all these models and impersonations are based?

Does Santa Claus actually exist?

The question is as old as civilization itself, and even older if you count early tribal peoples, who just wandered around, hunting and gathering and wishing and hoping and bitching and moaning and showing up to stay in places without a reservation. (Hence the importance today of Native American Indian reservations, to redress this grievous lack.) The range of opinions regarding Clausite existence spans the gamut, from the outright denial of Aclausites ("There is no such thing as Santa Claus.") to the fervent affirmation of the faithful ("Yes there is, and shut up."). Each side marshals its propositions, refutations, challenges, and "proofs." And yet, after just under six-point-two jillion years of human history, neither side has so far been able to dissuade the other, leaving both entrenched in their respective positions.

Can the deadlock be broken? Can the matter be resolved once and for all? And can it be done in a way that takes full advantage of the burgeoning market for mildly "spiritual" works that offend no one and make everyone feel great (even Jews)? Can it mention chicken soup, angels, Heaven, a day of the week, an old guy's nickname, and "code" in the title?

I believe that it can, except for the title part. (And even with that, I tried. This work's original title was *Thursdays with Izzie in Heaven: Santa Claus, Angels, and the Chicken Soup Code*. My priggish and shortsighted editor made me change it.) I hope, by bringing together all the most persuasive and enduring arguments in favor of Santa's existence, to prove conclusively that Santa Claus is a living presence, a gift-toting, reindeer-whipping reality.

Of course some will wonder, why undertake such a project? For those who believe Santa exists, no proof is necessary; for those who do not, no proof is sufficient. The answer, as it always is whenever someone wants to justify publicly doing something for their own private purposes, is: for the children.

If the events of 9/11 have taught us anything, it is that our children are our future. But if this is so, then it follows that *their* children are *their* future.

And yet our children have no children.

Which means our children have no future.

It is to assuage this dismaying state of affairs that the present work was written. For it is surely true that if our kids have no future, they do have disposable income. If every child on earth were to buy a copy of this book (after its translation into eighty-three languages and a print run into the hundreds of millions), and read it, and derive hope from it, I would be content.

But if they don't? Then let it be purchased for them by an entire generation of parents, grandparents, aunts, uncles, teachers, coaches, clergymen, pediatricians, social workers, babysitters, and well-meaning strangers. Let them purchase it for the same reason that I have written it: for the children.

Someone will say, "Yes, but I am Jewish, or Muslim, or Hindu, or of some other religion for which the figure of Santa Claus is at best a pathetic and risible fiction. Why should I care about, and purchase, the present work?" To him or her I say: The issue of Santa Claus's existence has ramifications that extend far beyond the interest of any particular religion or spiritual worldview. If Santa Claus exists, then he exists for all of us.

If, on Christmas Eve, he truly does bring presents for good little Christian boys and girls, then he is available to bring presents to everyone else, including good little non-Christian boys and girls and big, bad grownups, on the other 364 days of the year.

Someone will say, "Well, then, why doesn't he?" Perhaps because he hasn't been asked. Why has he not been asked? Because in order to ask something of someone, you first have to believe that that someone exists.

That is why I have written this work. Plus for the children.

One of the few known photographs of
Mrs. Claus. Here, exhausted Santa is greeted after
arduous Christmas Eve labors by his wife, who has
been drinking heavily. Rumors of marital tension
are an annual occurence.

CHAPTER ONE

The Ontological Argument[1]

I T is possible to imagine a perfect Santa Claus. But this perfection would not be complete if it did not include existence. Indeed, a Santa Claus who didn't exist

---

1 *Ontology* is the study of being, i.e., of that which exists as contrasted with that which does not exist. Thus, The Ontological Argument is the argument that holds that Santa Claus exists because he just has to, because if he didn't, he wouldn't be Santa Claus. Isn't that slick? But the reader is cautioned not to think too intently along these lines, lest he fall into the ontological error of believing that he himself (or she herself) is Santa Claus. And that is absurd. Not every reader of this book can be Santa Claus. That is a privilege reserved for only one very special reader. Hi, Santa!

would not *be* perfect—for, if he did not exist, then no matter how jolly, fat, and generous he was, how could he bring us presents?

Therefore, the perfect Santa Claus, because we can imagine him, *must* exist.

ELABORATION OF THE
ONTOLOGICAL ARGUMENT

It is not only possible to imagine the perfect Santa Claus, it is very easy to do so. Indeed, I am doing so right now. See?

All right, admittedly, at that moment I was not imagining a perfect Santa Claus. I was imagining myself playing strip miniature golf with Charlize Theron. Why? Because it amuses me. But all I need do is replace that imagining with a conception of the perfect Santa Claus. As I will do, with the swiftness of thought, at once.

It would seem that I am not disposed to do so at this moment. Nonetheless, if I *were* able to think of something besides a seminude Charlize Theron (holding a putter—no, holding *my* putter—posing fetchingly in front of a scale-model castle), I could quite easily conceive of a perfect Santa Claus.

Let the reader imagine that I have done so. Or let the

reader do so him- or herself, if the reader is so smart. In any case, there he is: the perfect Santa.

Everyone knows what he looks like; even small children, who know almost nothing, know that the perfect Santa Claus is fat, jolly, and Caucasian.[2] He has a long white beard. He wears a red suit trimmed in white fur and a red floppy conical hat topped with a white pom-pom. (It has often been asked, "A red suit trimmed in white fur and a red floppy conical hat topped with a white pom-pom? Are you suggesting that the perfect Santa Claus is gay?" No. Santa Claus is not gay—although his being perfect exists entirely apart from his being not gay. It *simply happens to be the case* that Santa Claus is heterosexual. Indeed, he enjoys a committed

---

2 While this manuscript was circulating for informal review among the American community of santologists, the author received an indignant communication from the Coalition for the Advancement of Thin Morose Latinos, accusing him of weightism, moodism, and racism. "Why," the letter read, "must it automatically be assumed that the perfect Santa Claus is fat, jolly, and white? We call upon the author, the editor, and the publisher to amend the text to acknowledge the contribution that thin morose Latinos have made to American society, and to cite the possibility that the perfect Santa Claus could possibly be one of their number." My reply—that a society in which thin morose Latinos sought cultural advancement at the expense of Santa Claus was not a society in which I cared to live—has thus far gone unanswered.

monogamous relationship with a woman.[3] He wears shiny black boots, which, like his belt, are probably made of patent leather, but he is still not gay.)

The perfect Santa Claus maintains his primary residence[4] at the North Pole, which is also, when he is not making deliveries, his place of business. And suddenly

---

[3] Santa's spouse is rather an enigma and cause for some suspicion. Even her name (Mrs. Claus) seems not quite right. Claus is not Santa's last name. Do saints even have last names? If not, how *does* one refer to the wives of the saints? We are left, perhaps, with Mrs. Santa Claus, as one would say Mrs. Spider-Man or Mrs. The Incredible Hulk. In any case, she, too, is Caucasian, in late middle age, with a cheerful round face and gray hair. As far as we know, she is Santa's first wife. But apart from that, what do we really know about her? What is her maiden name? Who are her people? Is she good for Santa? Is she really right for him? These questions, while important, are beyond the scope of the present discussion.

[4] We may ask: Does he own or rent? The traditional literature and Christmas songs do not say. Of course, it is the American Dream to own your own home, just as it is the American Daydream to own someone else's home and charge them rent, and it is the American Nightmare to own your own or someone else's home and have to replace the roof and furnace in the same fiscal year. But our inquiry into Santa Claus's existence will find itself severely hampered if we do not, at the outset, grapple with one disturbing fact:

It is possible that Santa Claus is not an American.

Naturally, this idea is hard to accept. A loud, fat man who barges into people's homes to flaunt his wealth by foisting upon them an

it strikes one: Could Santa be an Eskimo?[5] Could it be that he speaks with an Eskimo accent (whatever that means)? In fact, Santa not only speaks unaccented American English, he does so in orotund tones ("Me-r-r-r-ry Christmas!") and with mellow sonorities that often sound remarkably like those of Walter Cronkite. And, say what you will about Walter Cronkite, no one has ever mistaken him for an Eskimo.[6]

Thus Santa Claus the man. But our portrait of the

---

array of usually tacky, unnecessary commercial products—how can Santa Claus *not* be an American? Nonetheless, the documentation is inconclusive. We have no evidence of a birth certificate, high school diploma, Selective Service registration, driver's license, passport, or Blockbuster card. Further, it may be asked, as I have often asked and no one has bothered to answer: Just who owns the North Pole, anyway? Canada? Russia? Lapland? What *is* Lapland? Isn't it a discount notebook computer site on the World Wide Web?

[5] My editor informs me that we don't say "Eskimo" anymore. We say "Inuit." Fine. Look, I'm trying to prove, in a rigorous and academically responsible manner, that Santa Claus exists. I can't keep track of everything in the whole entire world. In any case, I certainly do apologize to any Eskimos I may have offended, assuming any are reading this, assuming they can read.

[6] Am I, therefore, suggesting that Santa Claus *is* Walter Cronkite? While such an assertion might be superficially appealing ("Wow!" someone will say. "Santa Claus is Walter Cronkite!"), it will raise more questions than it answers. For example: If it is established that

perfect Santa Claus would not be complete without a brief description of his principal professional activity.

He commands a sleigh pulled by reindeer—although whether they total eight or nine in number and whether or not the nose of one is a red lightbulb depends upon which song they're playing on the oldies station or which poem you're listening to on NPR on Christmas Eve. (I am something of a devotee of these recitations and have sent three separate e-mails to National Public Radio suggesting that, for a refreshing change of pace this upcoming season, they might wish to produce a rendition of "The Night Before Christmas" in Klingon. I have not yet received a reply.) The reindeer can fly.

Despite his morbid obesity, Santa is able to wriggle down and climb up chimneys in millions of houses all over the world, including those houses that do not have chimneys, and including those houses that are not houses because they're apartments. (Note, here, that in the Southern Hemisphere, December 25 arrives in the middle of summer. Santa therefore probably enters homes in South America, Indonesia, Australia, and

---

Santa Claus is Walter Cronkite, we are left to speculate on whether or not Dan Rather is the Easter Bunny. Well, granted, now that he has retired from network news, Dan Rather probably *is* the Easter Bunny. But then who is Tom Brokaw? The Tooth Fairy? That is ridiculous.

much of Africa not through chimneys but through air conditioners. It cannot be a pretty sight. Then again, Christmas isn't about pretty. It's about presents. So long as Santa gets inside with his deliverables, he's doing his job.)

He does this on a single night and escapes unharmed regardless of the presence, in wood-burning fireplaces, of fire or hot embers. He is capable of consuming an almost limitless supply of milk and cookies while still remaining conscious, ambulatory, and lucid. And, despite violating every AMA-sanctioned standard of cholesterol level and sugar intake, he performs this feat year after year, never once posing a hazard to his reindeer team or imposing an aerodynamic deficit on his sleigh.

But these are secondary in importance. What makes him perfect—what makes him Santa Claus, and not just another overweight celebrity seeking exposure on talk shows—is that he brings presents.

He doesn't stand at the entrance to a department store, ringing a bell and extorting us, with his silent suffering, to put money in a pot. He doesn't hold court at a mall, dandling young children in his lap and mumbling, with insulting condescension, "Oh, wow! You'd like a GameCube! Awesome!" before reeling off to the men's room for a snort of Southern Comfort from a hip flask. He doesn't waltz coyly around an office handing out Christmas bonus checks and basking in the gratitude of the recipients as though it's his money he's giving away.

That's what the pretend Santas do. Not for the real Santa those acts of egotistic vainglory. The One True Claus, the Claus worthy of our worship and veneration, comes in when the kids are asleep, leaves the gifts under the tree, and exits. *Finis*.

Thus the portrait of the perfect Santa Claus. It seems familiar because it *is* familiar: deeply familiar, archetypal in its every detail. This, indeed, is the Platonic ideal of a Santa Claus and matches perfectly the description of Santa Claus that Plato himself gave c. 359 B.C. in the dialogue in which Socrates and Plato discuss the true meaning of Christmas.

It is, however, not quite complete. It lacks one final attribute: existence.

A Santa Claus who possesses all of the qualities and appurtenances discussed above nonetheless remains distinctly *imperfect* if he does not exist.

We can demonstrate this with what I (and Einstein) call a "thought experiment." Imagine two identical Santas. Each possesses the full complement of cardinal Clausal features: jolliness, generosity, the prestigious North Pole address, etc. The only difference between them is that one exists and the other does not.

Which is the more perfect? The answer is obvious. You can have Santa-like qualities up the ying-yang, but if you don't exist, you'll always be second-best to the man who does. (Note: I do not actually know what "the ying-yang" is. I suspect there is no such thing, that the preceding term is simply a colloquial expression. I employ it to augment this book's appeal to the young people, for many of whom the issue of Santa's existence is a matter of urgent debate, as several have repeatedly assured me.)

Thus, perfection, in the case of Santa Claus, demands and indeed requires existence.[7] And since we can (as we have already proven) imagine and conceive of such a perfect Santa, then therefore Santa Claus must exist.

---

7 Of course, existence per se does not bestow perfection and is itself no guarantee of perfection. A lot of things exist, most of which are demonstrably imperfect. One need only look at my vacuum cleaner to know that this is true.

Similarly, a large number of people exist; indeed, it would be almost impossible for a normal human being, however equipped with a broadband computer connection and Google links to a million research sites, to compile a definitive list *merely of the people who exist in the state of Delaware*. And yet many more exist. There are forty-nine other states in the United States, plus territories and possessions and pseudo-dominions such as Guam and Paradise Island and Epcot, plus quasi-municipalities such as Shoe Town, Hamburger Hamlet, and Circuit City, and other countries in the world.

Clearly, we live in a universe replete with people who exist—and, much as we may deplore many of them (e.g., the man who sold me my vacuum cleaner), this is not necessarily a bad thing. Yet all of these people, no matter how much they exist, are imperfect because, as everyone knows, "nobody's perfect."

Santa, rushing to make Christmas Eve deadline,
mistakenly enters home of a family of animals.
Time-pressure to deliver all presents to all eligible
homes in one night often resulted in such blunders,
but recent refinements in GPS technology
promise to alleviate these and similar difficulties.

CHAPTER TWO

The Causal Argument

EVERYTHING in our experience, in both the animate and the inanimate worlds, must have a cause, from the lily of the field to the sparrow of the sky to the chicken of the sea. When we ask ourselves, "What is the cause of Christmas?" we have an immediate and strong intuition that we haven't the faintest idea. Then, when we ask someone who knows, the answer is, "Christmas presents," since it wouldn't be Christmas without presents.

But we then find ourselves confronting an even more puzzling conundrum, a huge, orderly, and astoundingly well-coordinated spectacle that cries out for explanation. What causes Christmas presents? And, even more striking and "weird," what causes them to appear (a) all over the world, (b) under identical trees, and (c) at the same time?

This is an effect that can only be explained by a single cause, i.e., Santa Claus. It must then follow that Santa Claus exists.

ELABORATION OF THE
CAUSAL ARGUMENT

When a given thing can be attributed to a variety of possible causes, the principle of parsimony obtains.[1] As classically and confusingly enunciated by William of Occam (1285?–1349? Anyone—?), the principle of parsimony states that the probable and most likely explanation for any given phenomenon will be the least complicated.

---

1 Don't you hate that? "Obtains"? So do I. But my editor urged me to say things like that to lend this book "authority." I told him, "I got ya 'authority' right heah," and gestured toward my genital region. But he failed to respond. Why? I adduce two reasons: One, because we were on the phone. Two, since he hasn't paid me enough so that I could afford one of those clever camera phones that everybody but me is using these days, I was unable to transmit to him a

Yes, of course: "Duh." But in the fourteenth century certain things—the principle of parsimony, the concept of the double play, the importance of flossing—were not as obvious as they are today.

To illustrate the principle, let's take a common scenario familiar to us all from everyday life:

A Ferrari F430 is parked in front of a dermatologist's office. On its roof is a cheese Danish.

Two obvious questions arise. (1) Who drives a Ferrari to a doctor's appointment? (2) How did the pastry get there? Let us, for the moment, and probably forever, skip over the first question. With regard to the second, many possible explanations immediately come to mind:

1. The Danish was dropped by a passing bird. It fell onto the roof of the most expensive car in town—

---

photographic depiction of this amusing, admittedly somewhat racy quip.

I am also, it must be said, not crazy about the word *parsimony*. It reminds me of a number of other words that have nothing to do with the subject at hand, such as *parson*, *parsnip*, and *sanctimony*. Thus, "The parson spoke about the parsnip with great sanctimony." What, the reader may wonder, does this have to do with Santa Claus? Exactly nothing. So let's move on.

cheese side down, probably—because that's just how life is.

2. Extraterrestrials, possibly invisible to human sight, used their matter fabrication ray to create the car and the Danish, and to place them in front of the office. Indeed, they may also have created the office as well. The dermatologist may himself (or, "himself") be an alien.

3. The Ferrari, sprinkled with magic dust by the Blue Fairy from *Pinocchio*, came alive! And it decided it needed an appointment with a dermatologist. As soon as it arrived at the doctor's office, someone accidentally left a cheese Danish on the car's roof. Perhaps it was Charlize Theron, in an absentminded flush of excitement after our game of strip miniature golf and the unforgettable (albeit imaginary) events of the fourteenth hole (par 3, "Dutch-type windmill").

All of these explanations are at least superficially plausible. (True, they have absolutely nothing to do with Santa Claus, but if the reader will be patient, we'll get back to Santa soon. And frankly, if the reader won't be patient, perhaps this book isn't for him. Perhaps he should go read Apple Jacks boxes or Cancun brochures, which are probably more his speed.) These answers all deal with the question before us. And at first we are tempted to accept one of them, according to our individual personalities, worldviews, and fantasies involving beautiful blonde actresses and miniature golf.

But watch how quickly all of them are revealed to be unlikely, improbable, and ultimately insufficient, when compared to a much simpler theory:

4. The owner of the Ferrari had an appointment with his dermatologist. He was late, and so ate his breakfast—a cheese Danish—en route to his car. Before getting into the car, *he placed the cheese Danish on its roof in order to use both his hands to defend himself against attacking thugs.* Once he had successfully done so, he forgot the Danish was on the roof and simply got into the car and drove to the doctor's office.

This, we instantly see, is the most likely explanation. Yes, the first three hypotheses *could* account for the scenario under discussion, but now that we think of it, we find we are able to "pare away" various elements of each as being simply too contrived or unlikely. A bit of common sense proves decisive: most birds, after all, don't buy cheese Danishes. They lack the requisite taste and are more than happy with Sno Balls, Ho Hos, Ding-Dongs, Yodels, and Twinkies.

As the car wasn't parked in Area 51, where the aliens

live, how likely is it, really, that extraterrestrials are involved in this whole situation?

And everybody knows that automobiles, even Italian sports cars magically endowed with life, simply have no need of dermatological care.

But people eat cheese Danishes, put things on their car roofs, and use both hands to defend themselves, their cars, and their baked goods all the time.[2]

Thus, we apply Occam's razor to whittle away the extraneous, less likely causes of a thing to arrive at the simplest explanation consistent with the available empirical evidence—a procedure that proves especially powerful when applied to Christmas. (And, yes, to Santa Claus. Happy now?)

Every Christmas the same remarkable scenario unfolds: "Magically," billions of Christmas presents appear under millions of Christmas trees across the nation and around the globe.

How is this possible? What is its cause? Our first im-

---

2 Of course, someone may challenge this explanation with, "Oh yeah? Well how come the Danish didn't fall off during the ride?" But we may easily dispense with this objection by citing the profound and well-known stickiness of pastry icing. "But cheese Danishes don't have icing," someone will whine. No, they don't. They have cheese. Which is also sticky, or at least mildly adhesive.

pulse is to assume, "It's just an amazing coincidence." But, seriously. I mean, really. Come *on*.

The suggestion that more than a billion strangers, without consultation or coordination, just happen to wrap overpriced toys, ill-chosen sweaters, plaques displaying singing fish, and last-minute bottles of contrived liqueurs in garish gift paper and *simultaneously*— place them under hundreds of millions of small pine trees (or horrible aluminum approximations thereof) is just frankly absurd. Because think about it. Plus the trees themselves are all decorated with the same things! With balls and tinsel and candy canes and angels and little cookie men. How can this possibly be a coinci dence? And even if such a fantastic concurrence could take place once, what are the odds of such a thing occurring year after year? At exactly (more or less) the same time? How is it that there has been no media coverage of this astounding event?

And yet, if the occurrence of Christmas cannot be ascribed to a yearly coincidence, neither can it be attributed to the opposite of a coincidence, namely, a conspiracy. Imagine the logistics required. Every single person who celebrates Christmas would have to be flown or driven—in secret—to a single place to discuss the plan and receive their orders. Where would everyone meet? Who would be in charge? Who could possibly cater such an event? What convention center in the world has adequate parking for the two billion cars of the earth's estimated two billion Christians? (Source: http://www. adherents.com/Religions_By_Adherents.html)[3]

A far simpler and therefore more likely explanation is not that billions of men and women somehow, by chance or coordination, do the same thing at the same time every Christmas, but that one man does this one thing, two billion times, very fast. Per Occam's dictum (a phrase I particularly like, even if no razor is involved), by reducing the causative agent behind Christmas to a single person, in a stroke we eliminate having to explain the parking and the catering and so forth.

Moreover, psychologically this explanation makes a lot of sense. Why? Because it involves the opposite of paranoia.

As even my editor knows, paranoia is the mental dysfunction in which the subject ascribes malign intent to those around him (or her). Everyone looks suspicious; everyone is endowed with the will and the power to do the subject ill. Strangers, we feel, want to kill us. People on the bus can't wait for us to get off so they can

---

[3] Granted, many people, especially spouses, will double up for the trip. There would, to an extent consistent with keeping the whole thing secret, be car pools. Call it one billion cars. Still, what parking lot can accommodate a billion cars without attracting attention, and without dooming those who forgot where they parked to wander around for weeks before perishing from exhaustion and hunger?

burst into derisive laughter. We are certain that our dog is in league with the Libyan secret police.

Now, naturally, we sane people have all felt these fears at one time or another. But thank God we usually can reassure ourselves that it's crazy! Note here that the evil intent that the paranoid individual ascribes to others actually originates in him. He (the one) projects it onto others (the many) and as such it is, as we say, "nuts."

But with the causal argument we have employed a rationale that is the opposite of paranoia. We have ascribed the will and the power (to give two billion Christmas presents) to a single person. We have reduced the many *to* the one. It's the inverse of paranoia, and therefore the opposite of crazy and nuts. It's sane! So it must be even more true.

But if we have proven that Christmas presents and Christmas itself are caused by one person, we find ourselves confronting a new conundrum: who?

What single individual is capable of selecting, wrapping, and distributing the gifts that endow Christmas with its very existence? Who has the time? Who has that much available room on their credit cards? Who has that much patience to deal with all that wrapping paper, which wrinkles so damned easily, and all those ribbons, which are such a pain, and all those little prefab bow thingies? And who, dear God, has access to that much Scotch tape?

The answer is, of course, no one. Such a proposition is ludicrous. Struggling with the wrapping paper alone can drive any normal human being into a murderous rage, as I can attest from repeated personal experience.

But to put the question thus is to fundamentally misunderstand the nature of Christmas. For it is not the selecting and the wrapping of the gifts that matter here. Those tasks, vital though they are, may be assigned to surrogates and assistants. What matters, what must be so if Christmas is to be sufficiently caused, is the appearance of all the gifts under all the trees, all on the same magical, mystical night.

Our question, then, becomes: Who is capable of delivering the gifts (selected and wrapped by others—probably elves) to the many households where Christmas is celebrated each year?

Before attempting an answer, let's review what qualities such a person must necessarily possess:

1. *This person should probably be a male.*

   Reason: The task requires immense physical strength and endurance, and all men are stronger than all women, with the exception of those who are not. Moreover, this person will be called upon to enter hundreds of millions of homes, alone, on Christmas Eve, and it is simply the case that a lone, unaccompanied woman seeking entrance at night to the homes of strangers often arouses suspicion, fear, and moral disapproval.[4] Such a reaction would severely hamper this person's ability to perform her task.

An unaccompanied man, however, could just be a chimney sweep on work release, or a political pollster, or a particularly zealous FedEx delivery guy, and will thus occasion a minimal outcry.

2. *This person—a man—must have an extraordinary means of transportation.*

Reason: He will be called upon to move rapidly and efficiently from rooftop to rooftop—something no ordinary car or bicycle or even helicopter can do. Of course, everyone knows that in the future we will all have individual jet packs that will enable us to fly wherever and whenever we wish. But, while we often like to comfort or flatter ourselves with the thought that the future is now, the brute truth is, the future is not now. The present is now. The future is later—in some cases

---

[4] "What kind of woman," many people invariably say to each other on such occasions, "goes from house to house in the middle of the night, climbing down chimneys? She must surely be either a prostitute, a lesbian, or some unsavory refugee from a fake reality show. Quick, call the police or some other similar authority."

much later. We don't have individual jet packs. Therefore, the man in question must have at his disposal some other, unorthodox method of transport.

3. *He must be fat.*

Reason: The job entails the delivery of literally tons of toys and other gifts to billions of homes on a single night. It is a rigorous, demanding challenge that allows little time for snacks. Thus, the man who performs it must have a reserve of body fat capable of being metabolized into energy if, for whatever reason, he falls behind schedule and must skip a break. Also, many of the homes he visits are located in places with cold winter climates. A layer of insulating body fat thus confers a distinct benefit.

4. *It would be advantageous if he were Christian.*

Reason: While not strictly a logical requirement— a Jewish, Muslim, Hindu, or other non-Christian man would, in physical terms, be equally as capable of delivering Christmas presents as a Christian man—nonetheless he stands a much higher chance of success with his mission if he is, indeed, a Christian. He would be more apt to be welcomed by the Christians whose homes he would so peremptorily attempt to enter. Indeed, they would assume he *was* a Christian. Were he not, each of his visits would probably have to be preceded by a shouted disclaimer[5] that would both threaten to wake the children and, repeated millions of times, tax the gift-bringer's voice to the point of inaudibility.

Based on these four criteria alone, our hypothesis is apodictic ("clearly proven or demonstrated; incontestable"—*The American Heritage Dictionary of the English Language*). Christmas is caused by a single bringer of gifts. This individual must be a fat Christian male with an unusual form of transportation. Only Santa Claus fulfills these requirements.

Therefore, Santa Claus exists.

---

5 E.g., "Hey guys! I'm here with your Christmas presents! But I'm a secular Zoroastrian, FYI!"

Scene from early (1870) television commercial for
Clagson's Mud and Grass Christmas Pudding Ball.
Tag line: "Repellent it may be, but at least it
is not fruitcake."

CHAPTER THREE

The Argument from Design, or the Teleological[1] Argument

CHRISTMAS is a nonrandom event. It shows clear signs of having been designed for a number of specific purposes. These purposes conform exactly to the salient characteristics, talents, and abilities of Santa

---

1 No doubt the reader is frightened by this word. That is as it should be. Fields such as philosophy, theology, and Santa theory deal in pure abstractions; the only way to judge the importance and competence of the people who work in them is by how scary their language is.

Claus. It is as though Christmas had been designed *for* Santa Claus—which would be impossible if Santa did not exist.

In addition, Santa Claus is the only figure well-suited (in red, with fluffy white fringe, available for Santa fans at Big 'n' Tall 'n' Immense 'n' Obese stores everywhere) to embody Christmas. Yet it is absurd to imagine that so important a holiday has been created to be incarnated in a being that does not exist.

Therefore, from both the purposes of Christmas being what they are, and from the success of Christmas at achieving those purposes, we can conclude that Santa Claus must exist.

ELABORATION OF
THE ARGUMENT FROM DESIGN

When we consider Christmas, wherever we look we see evidence of design—cute little reindeer on gift paper, pretty snowflake patterns on sweaters, etc. On Christmas cards we may quite commonly see a design of winsome angels, or of smiling stars, or similar adorable things. Of course, none of these designs is sufficient to confirm the reality of Santa Claus. Even the design of a series of tiny jolly Santa Claus faces on festive holiday napkins is no proof of his existence. It is, to be sure, proof of the existence of napkins. But is the existence of napkins, at this late date, in any real doubt? Surely not.[2]

If, however, we turn our attention from textile designs to a different meaning of *design*, that is, to the conscious and deliberate creation of something for a purpose, the discussion becomes more fruitful. (This idea of existing for a purpose is what is meant by teleology, hence, "The Teleological Argument." I encourage the reader and his or her friends and family to use this word in everyday conversation. For example, instead of saying to the idiot teenage employee at Best Buy, "What the hell is the point of a cell phone that works

---

2 It should be noted here that the entire foregoing discussion of design is irrelevant to the topic under consideration. And yet, tough. I introduce it to make a point. Say, hypothetically, I engage in a shouting argument with my aesthetically myopic (and ethically constipated) editor over his reluctance to wear the perfectly nice necktie I bought him as a Christmas present during the time he was considering purchasing the present manuscript. Let us further stipulate that this tie was decorated with a delightful pattern of fairyland sprites— a motif fully in keeping with the season and that I personally found quite charming. Suppose, rather than react as any civilized, sophisticated person would (i.e., "It's wonderful. Thank you so much."), he adopted a two-pronged position toward this gift: that my giving it to him was (a) "highly unprofessional and a little weird" and (b) "creepy." (And say that I subsequently learned that he just hated it, which would, of course, constitute a third prong.) Let us further suppose that I defended, quite vigorously, both the giving of a

underwater?" try saying, "What the hell is the *teleology* of a cell phone that . . ." I'm sure you'll be pleased with the twofold result: You get to display, casually and without artifice, an impressive erudition; and you get to put a gibberish-spouting schoolboy nitwit in his place. When admiring bystanders ask, "Where on earth did you learn to speak like *that*?" merely answer, "Oh—from that Santa Claus book. All the bright young things are reading it this season. Surely you have, too?") Let us, therefore, focus on the teleology of Christmas.

Does Christmas have a purpose?

Christmas is, ostensibly, a celebration of the birth-

Christmas gift to someone in whose hands I place my entire nascent career as a popularizer of santological theory, and the actual gift. That is to say, I spoke with sincere ardor about the cuteness of the little sprites. If, as is quite feasible, he were to laugh out loud and dismiss the pattern of the tie as "unbelievably hideous," and I were to contradict him, and we were to raise our voices in dispute over the phone, then in such an instance one would say that we were engaged not in an argument from design but in an argument *about* design. The confusion of one with the other originates in the ambiguous, dual meanings not only of the word *design*, but of *argument*. Indeed, so many words in English are so replete with multiple meanings (e.g., *creepy*), it is a wonder anything can be discussed with any precision at all. That, added to the insensitivity of those ungrateful individuals charged with acquiring books like this for publication, makes the task of writing such works as the present one especially onerous. I don't know why I bother. But someone has to, so I do.

day of Jesus Christ. As such it purports to honor His values and teachings, which include but are not limited to: God's love for mankind and, especially, for the poor; humility before God and man; the abjuration[3] of material wealth and possessions; the need for commitment to God's agenda; the need to repent one's sins before God; the Golden Rule; and the need to forgive those who have sinned against one.

In the face of such a list of Jesus' main tenets, we are drawn inexorably to inquire, *What the heck does any of that have to do with Christmas?!*[4]

In fact, nothing. Indeed, the closer we examine Christmas, the more we penetrate to what we might call its irreducible commerciality and break it down into its

---

3 Abjuration is a slightly more elegant way of saying *repudiation* or *renunciation*. The reader may be thinking, *Why would he use such a word in this text, when he certainly doesn't use it in real life?* But I do use it in real life. Only last week I had occasion to say, to some yammering bonehead employee at Best Buy, "If my life has stood for anything, it has been the abjuration of making phone calls underwater." The reader should have seen that young man's face!

4 I think I may state, without undue boasting, that there is probably no work in the canon of Western philosophical inquiry that contains a sentence ending in ?! with the possible exception of some (typically overheated) journal entries by Nietzsche and Spinoza's famous recipe for Chanukah doughnuts. Similarly, there is probably no usage in the standard santalogical texts of the word *heck*. I employ both

constituent elements, the more we see that its method of honoring the teachings of Jesus is to slap them across the face and laugh raucously in their face!

Let us consider these aspects of Jesus' teachings one by one:

a. *God's love for mankind and, especially, for the poor*—Christmas (with its stresses and insults, its jammed parking lots and mobbed stores, its wretched weather at the very time in which the kids are home from school, its jacked-up airline prices and frequent flier blackout dates, and its horrible, horrible movies) cannot possibly be said to represent or honor (or even provide much evidence of) God's love for mankind. No deity who loved mankind would display that love with a holiday in which a program on which Dolly Parton and Kenny Rogers sing "Walkin' in a Winter Wonderland" is considered a "special." As for God's love for the poor, it is difficult to think of a

---

of these unconventional tropes without apology. If the professional philosophers—with their endowed chairs, their tenure, their teaching assistants, their cushy office hours, and their adoring, lissome grad students—wish to object, let them. I have chosen a different path. I choose to write for ordinary people, people who have to work for a living, who know what the heck an exclamation point is! And aren't afraid of it! Okay?!

single other holiday so guaranteed to make the poor *feel* poor. Indeed, everyone is called upon to feel even sorrier for the poor during Christmas, because it *is* Christmas. So forget this one.

b. *Humility before God and man*—Please. The awarding of Christmas bonuses and vacations, the gifting of presents (or the presenting of gifts, or however we're now supposed to say it), and other, similar holiday rituals surely can have no other effect on an individual than the amplification of the *opposite* of humility. I don't know about the reader, but when someone hands me a check for $850 and/or a membership in the Fruit of the Month Club, the last thing I feel is *humble*. As for the children, we are talking about a three-week orgy of Christmas candy, holiday treats, seasonal snacks, special desserts, and bonus num-nums, plus presents, trips, outings, parties, *Nutcrackers, A Christmas Carols,* and a series of audiences with one or another ersatz Santa, to whom they recite a list of what they want as though reading from a ransom demand. And you dare cite humility?

c. *The abjuration of material wealth and possessions*—The ways in which Christmas celebration flouts this value are, really, too clichéd to be worth mentioning. To modern capitalist society, the period between Thanksgiving and Christmas Day has become the equivalent of what the harvest was for our ancient Sumerian friends: a time of hoped-for bounty, eagerly monitored signs and portents, and public expressions of triumph or defeat in the face of a good or bad season—in our case, yes, a *shopping* season. To indulge in the vernacular, don't get me started, because I'm not going there.

d. *The need for commitment to God's agenda*—How many times have we heard someone, during the Christmas season, say, "God's agenda? Yeah, right. Meanwhile, I have my own agenda. I have a ton of shopping to get done and thirty people coming over this Friday. I was going to make lamb. Can you get lamb? Does lamb even *exist* in December? Jesus Christ, what time is it? I'm late for my nail appointment." To ask the question is to know the answer.

e. *The need to repent one's sins before God*—Dream on, God.

f. *The Golden Rule*—Actually, this is the one Christian tenet ("Do unto others as ye would have them do unto you.") that people end up honoring, in however distorted and farcical a way. You think of buying for X, a second-tier colleague for whom you must get *something*, a box of lavender-scented soaps. You reason, "Well, I wouldn't mind getting that." You have invoked the Golden Rule, however pathetically and self-servingly.

g. *The need to forgive those who sin against one*—This, perhaps the most Jesus-like of all the precepts, is the most difficult to enact under the best of circumstances, let alone during the holidays. Why? Because during the holidays everyone is subject to an additional societal pressure not present during the rest of the year: the pressure to *be happy*. It is almost impossible to forgive those who sin against one while under such stress. One doesn't think, "I forgive you," but rather, "Stop sinning against me! My Visa's maxed out and I just remembered I have to get lavender-scented soaps for what's-his-name, and I'm not happy!"

What more need be said? What more need be demonstrated? As a birthday tribute to the teachings of Jesus, Christmas is a fraud.

In fact, the very essence of Christmas consists of feeling coerced into spending inordinate sums of money, giving insufficiently appreciated presents and receiving inadequately considered gifts in return, arranging laborious and expensive parties or attending the emotionally extortionate parties of others, getting drunk at the office, kissing the wrong person or no one at all, and in some way embarrassing oneself, screaming at one's children, and succumbing to depression—while, throughout, proclaiming that it is "the happiest time of the year" and "a celebration of peace."

Furthermore, not only has Christmas virtually nothing to do with Jesus' teachings, it bears absolutely no resemblance to His, or anyone else's, birthday.

For one thing, regardless of where Christmas is celebrated the world over, there is no birthday cake. On the contrary, the cake most commonly associated with the holiday is the fruitcake, a confection so starkly opposite in every way from a birthday cake as to constitute its Evil Twin, or an anti–birthday cake. Some physicists have theorized that if a standard-sized birthday cake and a fruitcake were to come into close physical proximity, their mutually antagonistic cake energies would draw them inexorably together into one highly reactive mass, creating an explosion on a par with the big bang itself and effectively destroying the known universe. No attempt has been made to verify this hypothesis experimentally, for obvious reasons.

At this point someone will say, "Oh God, he's going to make fun of poor old fruitcake now. Talk about beating a dead horse!" I am, yes—both because it supports my thesis, and because I have recently figured out how to create a table in Microsoft Word, and this topic offers me a fine opportunity to do so.

A birthday cake is light in texture, frothy, and soft. The typical fruitcake is the color of tree bark, is as compacted and dense as midfield at Giants Stadium, and possesses the texture of half-cured concrete studded with baked rubber grommets. A birthday cake makes a pleasant platform for the display of candles. It is impossible to plant candles, or indeed anything not made of drop-forged steel, in a fruitcake.

A graphical representation of the similarities and differences between birthday cake and fruitcake can be seen in Diagram 1, a table I myself created in Microsoft Word.

Clearly, speaking in strictly cake-o-logical terms, Christmas is no one's birthday.

The songs of Christmas also belie its pretense at celebrating Christ's birthday. Of the many hundreds of traditional and contemporary Christmas songs, carols, and hymns, not once does anyone sing "Happy Birthday to You," surely the sine qua non of birthday songs. "Silent Night" is a beautiful song, but the last thing you want to do, having sung it, is to make a wish, blow out candles, and give anyone, anywhere, a pinch to grow an inch.

Finally, if Christmas were really Jesus' birthday, then, in accordance with a well-known tradition, we would give Him presents. He is, as it were, the Birthday Boy of Boys and we are the celebrants. Instead, like the members of a lunatic cargo cult for whom a once-sensible practice has been warped by fear and irrationality, we engage in a mad orgy of giving gifts to

**COMPARISON OF BIRTHDAY CAKE AND
FRUITCAKE AS DISPLAYED IN A TABLE THE AUTHOR
HIMSELF CREATED IN MICROSOFT WORD**

	Birthday Cake	Fruitcake
Yummy?	Yes	No
Goes well with		
coffee	Yes	No
tea	Yes	No
milk	Yes	No
Scotch	No	No
water	Yes	No
Suitable for displaying messages?	Yes	No
Freshness measurable in . . .	Days	Geologic time
Holds candles?	Yes	No
Holds rebar?	No	Some *(38 inches long max.)*
Fluffy, moist, light?	Yes	No
Typical sheet cake feeds . . .	24	Australia *(NB: In theory only; no field data available)*
Alternate use	Anniversary cake	Traffic pylon anchor
Popular meaning	Beloved symbol of celebration and joy	Feared harbinger of holiday depression or gift-recipient disappointment

everyone *except* Him: family, friends, colleagues, clients, customers, the postman, the paperboy, and so on. We even, when we put a dollar in a Salvation Army pot, give gifts to total strangers.

It is thus incontestable that Christmas has nothing at all to do with the life, teachings, or birthday of Jesus Christ.

What, then, can possibly be its real purpose?

We finally may begin to uncover an answer by listing its most obvious, objective characteristics. Christmas, as everyone will agree:

a. *celebrates happiness itself.* Not all holidays do; in fact, no secular American holiday does. Rather, American holidays celebrate independence, thankfulness, presidents, mothers, fathers, ghosts and witches and pumpkins, veterans, soldiers who have died in wars, flags, and the labor movement. And trees. But just barely. For years I conducted a campaign to persuade this country to accord Arbor Day the respect it deserves, without success. Now even I have given up.

b. *is synonymous with gift giving.* Indeed, it institutionalizes gift giving: you feel compelled to give gifts (as noted above) to near strangers, not because of anything having to do with them, but because it is Christmas.

c. *is a religious holiday that has attained quasi-secular status.* Christmas pervades secular American culture like no other holiday. Rock bands and pop singers do not regularly issue Yom Kippur albums or Ramadan singles. Public schools do not close for Ash Wednesday vacation. American life is utterly silent about Buddhist holidays—I'm not even sure that there is such a thing as a Buddhist holiday, which of course further proves my point.

d. *commemorates and celebrates winter.* Even in places where winter can barely be said to exist, such as Los Angeles or the absurdly well-groomed gated communities of south Florida, people take it upon themselves to display Christmas trees and wreaths bedecked with "snow." It's all entirely artificial and pathetic, of course, but the point is: they make the effort.

While there may be others of lesser importance, these are the four principal characteristics of Christmas.[5] Indeed, so overwhelmingly do they define the

---

[5] Christmas may also be said to: (a) provide artificial support for the poinsettia, pine tree, and mistletoe industries; (b) celebrate/underwrite the U.S. Postal Service; (c) advance the interests of the eggnog and candy cane cartels; (d) provide what meager yearly stipend is

holiday, they may be said to constitute its raison d'être. They, and not some spurious combination of birthday bash and virtue fest, are its function and its purpose. Christmas, we see with a sudden thunderclap of insight, was *designed* to accomplish these four goals, because it so magnificently *does* accomplish them.

Any symbol or embodiment of Christmas must, therefore, be able to incarnate all of the functions just mentioned—to, yes, fulfill the *purpose* of Christmas. Does such a symbol exist? Is there anyone at all synonymous with (a) happiness, (b) gift giving, (c) religiosity turned secular, and (d) winter?

Clearly it is not Jesus, who can be eliminated on the strength of (a) alone, since He is never, ever shown smiling and, indeed, most depictions of Him focus on His agony. And while He may be said, somewhat, to embody the giving of gifts (loaves, fishes, sight, etc.), it is a secondary trait (and none of these quasi-gifts can be returned either for exchange, a full refund, or even store credit). As for (c), Christ stands for exactly the opposite, i.e., the secular imbued with religious

---

received by the surviving cast of *It's a Wonderful Life*; and (e) keep domestic tinsel factories on twenty-four-hour-a-day shifts for four weeks (late November to December 25), enabling them to sit idle the other forty-eight weeks of the year and still turn a tidy profit.

immanence[6] and significance. His connection with winter is moot, given that the only documentation we have of his life concerns his years in the arid deserts of the Middle East. That span between his late boyhood and his late twenties, when in fact Jesus may have loafed around the higher elevations or the mountains of that region as a ski bum or an amateur mountain climber, is lost to history.

No, in fact the only legitimate embodiment of Christmas is Santa Claus.

Think about it. Seriously.

He is entirely synonymous with happiness, as his well-known "Ho, ho, ho"™ (all rights reserved) attests. He is, in ways already enumerated, the Gift Giver Supreme. His public identity is ostensibly religious (he is a saint), but his actual role is, in fact, entirely secular. He is a saint in name only and utterly divorced from any of the characteristic qualities or events commonly associated with Christian saints, including terrible persecution, dreadful suffering, a ravaged appearance, and a torturous death. Finally, his association with win-

---

6 Immanence is an excellent word for impressing, not only one's boss, but single women. Anecdotes concerning the admiring looks the author has received for using it in various social situations (on line at a bank, on jury duty, etc.) are beyond the scope of this book— alas!

ter is absolute. For Heaven's sake, the man lives at the North Pole!

Thus Christmas, its teleology unambiguously established and proven, finds its absolute and perfect embodiment in Santa Claus.

We must now ask: Is it conceivable that so important and universal a holiday has been designed to be represented (so exactly!) by a figure that does not exist?

Of course not. Christmas being what it was designed to be, Santa Claus must exist.

Many "experiences" of Santa Claus are
actually of stand-ins, imitators, and surrogates—
many of whom are often dismissed by irate children
crying, "You're not Santa Claus!" In this photograph,
an embittered Claus impersonator cruelly runs
over a little boy. Note inauthentic horses.

CHAPTER FOUR

The Experiential Argument

MANY people have had a direct, personal experience of Santa Claus. Indeed, many have reported, with unquestionable sincerity, that they have sat on his lap. Moreover, they report that their lives were significantly changed by these encounters. Objective, third-party observation confirms many of these reports.

Since it is impossible to sit on the lap of a being who does not exist, and since it is impossible for one's life to be changed by a being who does not exist, and because so many people have claimed such experiences, Santa Claus must exist.

ELABORATION OF THE
EXPERIENTIAL ARGUMENT

At first this argument would appear to be the weakest of all those reviewed thus far. To begin with, it starts with what seems to be a solecism: a personal experience *of* Santa Claus. Shouldn't the preposition more properly be *with*?

After all, when we speak of having an experience of something, it is usually with regard to something abstract, e.g., "Susie had an experience of happiness" or "Dave had an experience of terror" or "I had a horrible experience of injustice when my editor suggested this chapter wasn't necessary."[1]

---

1 No doubt the reader thinks this example is fanciful and invented. I assure him or her that it was, and is, brutally real. "Might want to nix this," was my editor's scrawled comment at the top of chapter 4 on the proposal for the present work. "Seems thin." Thus, with seven curt words, is the labor of half a lifetime casually dismissed. Naturally, I returned the document to him (in person; or at least I tried to, although in the end I had to succumb to his assistant's repeated "He's in a meeting!" and leave it with her) with my response to his comment duly inscribed in indelible red marker: "Must keep. Will be fat."

I submit, however, that it is for this very reason that the phrase *experience of* with regard to Santa Claus is particularly appropriate. To have an experience of someone is to characterize that someone *as* a kind of abstraction, which is to say, in quasi-religious or spiritual terms.

An uplifting example: When, as I regularly do, I attend a performance by Celine Dion®[2] at Caesar's Palace in Las Vegas, I come away thinking, not, *I just saw Celine Dion®*, or, *I have just experienced Celine Dion®*, or even, *I have just experienced the Celine Dion® experience,* but, rather, *I have just had an experience of*

---

2 I append the registered symbol (®) after Ms. Dion's name after having seen it used, in just such a fashion, on a poster advertising her show at Caesar's Palace in Las Vegas, Nevada. I assume it serves some purpose other than mere affectation. Indeed, one can imagine a performer of Ms. Dion's caliber and accomplishment to be girded round with many legalistic safeguards and presentational requirements for sundry purposes. I consider this not only necessary but appropriate. If anyone deserves to transform her name into a federally protected entity enjoying a legal exclusivity guaranteed by the full faith and credit of the government of the United States, it is this diva. Plus, of course, she's Canadian, so she's probably living here to avoid the onerous taxes that the Canadian government levies in order to oppress its citizens with universal health care and other freedom-robbing programs. Beautiful, talented, and smart, truly she is my kind of woman!

Celine Dion®.[3] No other formulation will do justice to the event.

To speak of an *experience of* someone or something is to invoke the totality of the person or thing beyond any specific quality or attribute. We may, of course, have this or that experience *with* Santa Claus, e.g., "John had a pleasant experience bowling with Santa Claus," or, "After Kimberly's experience with Santa Claus she converted to Islam," or, "I saw Mommy having an experience with Santa Claus." But the individuals referred to at the start of this chapter—those who claim to have had an experience *of* Santa Claus—are referencing an

---

3 Indeed, the last time I saw *her*, she had an experience of *me*! Or she would have, if one of her people hadn't rudely torn from my grip the beautiful bouquet of roses I was attempting to deliver to her dressing room after the show, not only bruising the flowers but damaging my disguise (dress, high heels, wig, makeup, false breasts, etc.) to the point of uselessness. Granted, the reader might now be thinking, *What kind of experience of you could she have had if you had appeared before her disguised as a woman?* I had debated this, but in the end concluded it was the likeliest way to gain entry to the singer's dressing room. (If successful, I had planned to ask to use the bathroom, where I would remove my disguise and don the male clothes I had carefully packed into the capacious yet elegant evening bag I was carrying that evening.) I assumed the singer's bodyguards would (and regularly do) deny entry to an unauthorized man; I had hoped they would be more lenient and indulgent toward a woman. How wrong we can be!

altogether grander, more transformational, and more existentially significant thing.

Who are these individuals?

Most of them are children. Indeed, we would be surprised were this not the case, since children are to Santa Claus as schizophrenics are to psychiatrists, i.e., the former comprise the natural constituency of the latter. This analogy may be expressed in a more graphical form thus:

Children ◆ Santa Claus :: Schizophrenics ◆ Psychiatrists

This is not to imply that all children are schizophrenics or that Santa Claus is a psychiatrist. One could just as easily have rendered a different but equally valid analogy, e.g.:

Children ◆ Santa Claus :: Operagoers ◆ Pavarotti

This is a very powerful expression with equally powerful implications. Consider: Pavarotti is, within the larger population of adults, a leader in his field and world famous. So is Santa Claus. Thus we may expand the operation:

Santa Claus ◆ Adults :: Pavarotti ◆ Adults

And, since

Adults = Adults

Then it follows that

Santa Claus = Pavarotti
(QED)

I seem to have proven that Santa Claus is Luciano Pavarotti. This is not something I intended to do. [*Nor is it the purpose of this book.—Ed.*] I suppose I should assure the reader and my editor, who feels it necessary to intrude on my own disclaimer to offer a self-exculpating (and highly unnecessary) comment of his own, that I do not personally believe this to be the case, i.e., I do not believe Santa Claus and Pavarotti to be the same person. [*Then why write it?—Ed.*]

Someone will ask, "Then why write it?" The answer, of course—and as any editor familiar with the procedures of serious academic writing, as opposed to the denatured, imbecile-friendly works published for the popular audience, would know—is to follow the path of one's intellectual cerebration wherever it may lead. Naturally one doesn't expect an editor at a commercial publishing house to understand that, but still, one tries.

In fact, while finding that Santa and Pavarotti are the same person would conclusively prove the thesis of this book (since no one disputes the fact that Pavarotti exists), it would raise new questions not easily answered. Here are just a few, reprinted verbatim from my notes:

PRO
1. Both fat.

CON
1. Different-colored beards!

2. Does SC speak Italian? (NB: "Ho, ho, ho"™ int'l phrase common to many langs. Does SC get royalty?)

3. How poss. for P to appear in operas world over and live at N. Pole same time?

4. Q: DOES SC DRESS AND APPEAR AS SC ALL YEAR? Or only Xmas? Thus:

   ♦ Is P. Santa C's secret identity? (Cf. Clark Kent/Superman, etc.) Pro: allows global travel without arousing suspicion. Con: Where change into red suit w/furry trim? If dressing room at Met/La Scala/etc., then how unseen by well-wishers, bodyguards, entourage/people, theater staff, disguised fans arriving with roses, etc.?

5. If P is SC, who Carreras and Domingo? Santa's helpers?

6. What about others? Note marked scarcity of elves, reindeer at most operatic perfs. Mrs. Claus??

Let us, for now, concentrate on the more immediate and limited thesis that Santa Claus exists and set aside for future discussion the possibility that he is an internationally known operatic tenor. We return, then—as we must—to the children.

It is very common for children to have a personal experience of Santa Claus. Such reports, while admittedly rare during most of the year, proliferate wildly during the Christmas season.[4]

"We went to the mall and saw Santa." "Santa was at the store, and I sat on his lap and told him what I wanted for Christmas." "There was a long line and a lot of kids and everybody wanted to talk to Santa, so Daddy said fuck it and we had ice cream instead."

Moreover, a significant number of people who report a direct, personal experience of Santa Claus evince ob-

---

[4] Far from casting doubt on the validity of our argument, this fact actually reinforces it. If Santa existed, he would naturally be busy most of the year collecting and organizing the presents he brings during Christmas. In other words, a seasonal upswing in reports of Santa Clausal experiences is exactly what we would expect to encounter if Santa Claus existed. Only a Santa that didn't exist would be free to appear in public year-round.

jective, observable changes in their behavior during or subsequent to the event. They giggle. They look flushed with excitement. They grow very still and wide-eyed and are overcome with a devastating self-consciousness. Or they leap off Santa's lap and run crying like a big baby to their mommy.

And it is not only their demeanor that is altered. The very material conditions of their lives are also objectively, demonstrably changed. A girl who, since birth, has lacked Princess of Imperial Russia Barbie[5] discovers, often the very next day after her visit with Santa Claus, that that deficit has been corrected. The young lad who has longed all his life for the video game Murder Death Rampage Unlimited: Bloody Vengeance: A Time to Murderously Kill Everybody finds, a day or so after speaking with Santa Claus, that very title under his tree.

How, we might ask, can all this—these emotional responses, these physiological effects, the widespread granting of one wish after another—be possible via the agency of a being who doesn't exist?

---

[5] My editor, in a burst of useless pedantry, wrote: "Imperial Russia had Grand Duchesses, not Princesses; the princesses were minor royalty." Can the reader imagine the look on his face when I informed him that I obtained the name of this Barbie doll from a website devoted to Barbie collectibles? I can!

Of course, someone will point out that not every one of these experiences is of, or even with, the real Santa Claus. Many of the Santa Clauses visited and confided in by the above-referenced people are quite obviously faux Clauses, regular people dressed up to simulate Santa Claus. No doubt the reader knows people who have played Santa Claus at just such a mall, Christmas party, office function, etc. Indeed, the reader may have served as an ersatz Santa him- or herself![6]

Nonetheless, it is impossible not to be struck by the vast number of such reports. And even if most of them are erroneous—i.e., they describe an encounter with a

---

[6] My own experience in these matters is not without drama. Several years ago I was persuaded by a fellow santologist to whom I am no longer speaking to impersonate Claus at our annual Banquet and Awards Dinner. I was skeptical as to the appropriateness of this prank, but was assured by this individual that the group would be delighted to see me in full Santa regalia exactly because of the time of year (July 12) and the location of the event (the Fairmont Southampton Princess Resort in Bermuda). I arrived the night before the day of the dinner, and the next day spent a delightful time on the beach. Late in the afternoon I retired to my room to don the requisite false stomach, boots, red suit, white beard, pom-pom hat, etc. A quick phone call to the desk brought the information that the event was to be held in The Mid-Ocean Amphitheatre, a splendid state-of-the-art facility reserved for larger gatherings. One can imagine the stares I drew, in my Clausian attire, as I made my way down the elevator and through the ground-floor corridors to the designated room. Per

Santa Claus who is not the authentic, actual Claus—the sheer quantity of the reports leads us to a reasonable and important conclusion: at least one of them has to be authentic.

It just stands to reason. Because look at how many there are.

To believe otherwise is to believe that millions of the world's children are all—*all*—some combination of mistaken, stupid, lying, and insane. Granted, most children are, in fact, wrongheaded, ignorant, untruthful lunatics. But all? Who would dare to suggest such a thing? About the children! Surely there is one child,

---

the original plan (to surprise the membership), I entered through the stage door behind the dais and unseen by the audience. As I neared the stage itself, I saw with satisfaction that the event had begun: the audience was in darkness, and someone was addressing the group. At what I thought to be a propitious moment I bounded out into view, calling "Ho ho ho! Who's having fun?" During that initial second, blinded by the lights and disoriented by the ensuing uproar, I noted, in a series of lightning-quick impressions I was simply unable to process, that the audience looked both older and less festive than I had anticipated. I saw not a single familiar face. Then, from the floor came strangled cries of dismay, expressions of outrage, and a scream. Apparently a woman had fainted and several men clutched themselves in a labored effort to breathe. It was not until the house lights had come up, two security guards had begun to escort me from the auditorium, and I was able to read the banner across the rear of the stage that I realized that the proceedings I had interrupted were not

somewhere, who is none of these, one child who is capable of giving an accurate, intelligent, truthful, sane report without fidgeting or squirming or using foul language. Let him or her step forward and tell us in a polite, clearly spoken way, with good manners and no "attitude," that he or she has met the actual Santa Claus, and this issue will be resolved once and for all.

Although not to everyone, alas.

Ever since the experiential argument for Santa's existence was first advanced, there have been those who have challenged and criticized it. Some take issue with its premise. Others find fault with its conclusions. Some of these people openly admit—brag, really—that they don't believe in Santa Claus and therefore do whatever they can to attack or discredit those who report firsthand experiences of or with him.

And yet, isn't it funny that no matter how much they deny Santa's existence, when Christmas rolls around

---

those of an annual colloquium of philosophers and scholars discussing the phenomenon of Santa Claus but rather a commemorative gathering of "Pioneers" from the founding of the state of Israel in 1948. The rest of my evening was spent tendering abject apologies to the board and membership of the organization whose solemn convocation I had so inappropriately interrupted. About the "friend" who had convinced me to mount such a farcical and embarrassing stunt and the desk clerk he had bribed to misinform me of the meeting's location, the less said, the better.

and they're at the home of a family with children, they're the first to ask any wee tot that happens by, "And what do you hope Santa Claus brings you?"

Some might call this hypocrisy and condemn it as hateful, dishonest, stupid, horrible, and bad. But I prefer to take a more generous stance. I suggest that this drastic inconsistency, this so-called hypocrisy, is not entirely the result of evil, cowardice, or selfishness so much as a consequence of understandable, forgivable human weakness. It is easy to scoff at traditional teachings and to be independent when your life seems stable and all is well.

How tempting it is, to be all modern and up-to-date and not believe in Santa Claus when everything is going great, and it's any time between January and November.

But then Christmas arrives. And suddenly the world is a very different place.

Then you are surrounded by children who want and expect presents. And you are forced to confront children who say with complete sincerity that they have met Santa Claus, have spoken to him, and maybe have even touched his garment. At those times even the most devout unbeliever will find himself subject to doubt. Can all these human beings—because, make no mistake, I consider children to be human beings—be wrong? Can decades of stories, greeting cards, wrapping paper, and seasonal pop hits be wrong? If fifty million Frenchmen can't be wrong, and some of them believe in Santa Claus, then there's that, too.

Nonetheless, during the balance of the year there are many who reject even the possibility of Santa's existence, and some of them focus their attacks on the experiential argument. They have traditionally advanced a series of challenges, which I include below, along with my replies.

1. Why are experiences of Santa Claus restricted to those who already believe he exists? If he is an objective reality, why don't people who don't believe in him have encounters with him, too?

REPLY: First, because Santa has no time to waste with people who don't believe in him, many of whom are not Christian and therefore don't make themselves available to him to begin with. Second, I believe that many such people *have* had experiences of Santa Claus but, due to the very reason that they don't believe in him, they failed to identify him as Claus! Instead, they think they've just met a fat man in a wacky red suit, eating snacks and handing out toys. Perhaps they believe him to be a homeless person lugging a sack containing all his earthly belongings. Perhaps—but why go on? There is no limit to people's ability to deny the truth when it conflicts with their assumptions. They "know" Santa Claus doesn't exist, period. No amount of evidence or argument can make them believe otherwise. I actually feel sorry for them.

2. Why are experiences of Santa Claus mainly restricted to children?

REPLY: Because—obviously—Santa's job is to bring presents to good little boys and girls. And what are boys and girls? *Children.* As everyone but the people who ask this question seems to know. Besides, so what? Is anything automatically not valid or real just because it happens to a child? What about breathing? Children breathe!

3. Does Santa exist just because children say he does? What if children say the Tooth Fairy exists? Are we then to infer that she does?

REPLY: The children in question don't say he exists; they say they've had a personal experience speaking with him. If millions of children from all over the world, for decades, reported similar experiences with the Tooth Fairy, then maybe— but never mind. You may infer anything you wish. I just think it's sad that, when there is a belief available to every single human being, a belief that would bring every individual great joy and happiness, some obstinately insist on rejecting and denigrating it.

4. A child tells us she has seen "Santa Claus" driving a Nissan Xterra down Main Street: does this, too, count as a first-person experience of Santa Claus?

REPLY: This is a valid challenge and never fails to put me in mind of an incident that concerned one of my nieces. She was around six years old at the time. She and her family were stopped at a traffic light. In the lane beside them, a young woman with long, dark hair sat in the driver's seat of a convertible beside an older woman, presumably her mother. The light turned green, and the convertible drove off. A few moments passed. Then my niece announced, "Yup! That's Pocahontas!" Of course, in reality, it was not Pocahontas, and we should have been in error to give credence to the little tyke's report that it was. Still, which of us has not, at one time or another, seen a young lady with dark hair and, if only for a second, thought her a Native American princess from the seventeenth century? Or—somehow, *somehow*—an animated character from a historically inaccurate but beloved Disney movie come to life? This happens to me all the time, and I must assume it happens to others.

But no one, not even a small child, can mistake Santa Claus. Who is to say that Claus does not in fact drive a Nissan Xterra when in town? Skeptics are free to reject such reports in any case. Their number is minuscule compared to the huge quantity of more credible reports.

In the end, the experiential argument is compelling but mired in its own subjectivity. If no single individual's first-person encounter with Santa can be necessarily believed, we must fall back on brute numbers. But the numbers are considerable—and all we need is one.

In a burst of naughtiness, young girl tries to
strangle Santa. Drawing was made by child's father,
who was hiding in nearby closet and sketching
the scene. He managed to intervene in time. Incident
is unusual as most attempts at Santacide are
perpetrated by males.

CHAPTER FIVE

The Argument from Morality

ONE of the chief functions and purposes of Santa Claus at Christmastime is to serve as moral arbiter of whether we have been good or bad.

His methodology for this helpful (if seasonal) protocol is well-known: He makes a list. He checks it twice. He finds out who, in his estimation, is naughty and who, in contrast, is nice.[1] He then awards or withholds presents accordingly.

---

1 What does it mean to be "naughty"? Experts differ. Aristotle, in *On the Nice*, described naughtiness as "that state of character in which virtue is not present, but rather has been replaced or, insofar as it never had a chance to take root, is obstructed, as the stone ob-

In addition, when we're told to be good in order to receive what we want for Christmas, we usually *are* good, for exactly this reason.

We would not be inclined—and might not be able—to be good in order to appease a being who does not exist. Nor could Santa himself make such persuasive and binding moral judgments about us if he did not exist. Therefore, for both reasons, Santa Claus must exist.

---

structs the plant's shoot, in its establishment by an inability or indifference to govern the desire toward behavior, deed, action, thought, utterance, or attitude most characterized by not being nice." Actually, Aristotle didn't say that. I did. I made it up. Still, it does capture a bit of Aristotle's tendency to yammer on and on. Consider, by way of contrast, Sartre, in chapter 3 of *Being and Naughtiness*: "We will call that condition in which Being thrusts itself unhesitatingly forward as Being-not-nice, *self-naughtiness*, to distinguish it from 'competing' naughty-modes in which the Other, fully confronted by Being's being-naughty, responds to Being *qua* naughtiness, which," Did you notice that I ended this sentence with "which" and a comma? I wonder if you did. I wonder if anyone reads these footnotes at all. Let us conduct a little experiment. I'm going to leave that sentence fragment from Sartre (which I also made up) as is, and

ELABORATION ON THE
ARGUMENT FROM MORALITY

Where does morality come from? Why do we care about being good? Why, when we do something bad, do we feel guilty about it, except when it's really someone else's fault, as it usually is?

Psychologists have their own vocabulary for discussing this phenomenon, of course, since they have their own vocabulary for everything because they think that they *know* everything. It was a psychologist, in fact, who labeled the philosophical inquiry into the existence and meaning of Santa Claus "a pseudo-academic exercise in faux spirituality and nitwit apologetics com-

---

we shall see if my editor even notices it. Oh, the copy editor will, make no mistake. But if the actual editor fails to point it out, I will insist the copy editor leave it in, and the reader will be able to tell if my editor actually did bother to edit the manuscript or was simply too busy having lunches and cocktails with other authors, agents, and colleagues to give the manuscript the attention it deserves. [*I noticed, yes. But I chose to take the moral high ground here and let this big baby have his little grammatical joke. Now let's get on with his long-winded footnote.—Ed.*] Finally, this, from Nietzsche: "But thus do I counsel you, my friends: distrust all in whom the impulse to punish is powerful!" This quote is authentic, but we read it with alarm. Is the famously cranky German philosopher here issuing a subtle condemnation of Santa Claus? Wouldn't *that* be typical!

bined with a lot of made-up, nutty, posturing bull-shit."[2]

But then, psychologists fear Claus, just as they fear everything transcendent, including God, Fate, and the existence of Absolute Naughtiness. Thus do they take our sense of right and wrong—the very thing that (along with the pledge to the flag and square dancing) separates us from the animals—and bestow upon it the juvenile, comic-book-hero name, the superego. I call it what the rest of the normal world calls it, namely the conscience.[3]

---

2 Some (drunk) person I met at a party, in conversation. In reply I—most eloquently, I thought—turned on my heel and walked out, not only of the room but of the entire apartment. The fact that the apartment and the party were mine only served to lend the gesture additional force, I think. To this day I do not know who the individual was or which of my invited guests brought him, but I am pretty sure he was a psychologist.

3 Although I affirm my contempt for the term used by psychologists to refer to our inner moral sense, I must say I am struck by what I think is a fine idea for a comic book adventure series. The protagonist is called Superego, and his superpower is the selfsame superpower that so effectively governs all civilized behavior; he uses his moral authority to persuade criminals to stop breaking the law. I have sketched out the dialogue for a model episode of the series. A sample scene:

Two hoodlums are robbing an armored car, holding its driver and guard at gunpoint. Superego arrives (via flight? Teleportation? TBD).

Why do we have a conscience at all? Why do we obey an inner impulse that tells us, often in the voice of Jiminy Cricket, to let our conscience be our guide? If we do let our conscience be our guide, is it necessary, after it has finished guiding, for us to give it a tip? We want to know, because we want to do the right thing. But why? Where does this internalized sense of obliga-

---

BAD GUY 1. Uh-oh. Oh no. Yikes. Oh Jeez. It's Superego.

SUPEREGO. Hold it right there, boys.

BAD GUY 2. Don't get in our way, Superego, or we'll shoot these helpless guys.

SUPEREGO. You're not going to do anything of the kind, my friend. You're going to put down your weapons and release those innocent individuals.

BAD GUY 2. Oh yeah? And why would we do that, buster?

SUPEREGO. Because robbing armored cars and holding people hostage and threatening everybody with guns is wrong. And, what is more, you know it is wrong. Don't you?

BAD GUY 1. Hey, he's got a point.

BAD GUY 2. Shut up, you. I don't care what's wrong. I want money, I tell you!

I'm not sure what happens next, but I will continue to work on the scenario. Meanwhile, if any competent artist wishes to team up with me to promote this project, he or she can contact me in care of my editor, who, considering his ill-natured comment about the above scene ["What the hell is this? You're supposed to be talking about Santa, not some superhero. Pay attention!"—*Ed.*] may be in for quite a surprise when he sees the amount of interest this idea generates.

tion, this capacity to behave morally the way your mother, clergyman, or parole officer always wanted you to, come from?[4]

There are various theories that attempt to answer this age-old conundrum and, not surprisingly, they vary according to which intellectual interest group puts them forward. The anthropologists claim that morality comes from the evolution of cultures and other anthropology-type things. (Coincidence?) The sociologists assert that morality comes from society—*which just happens to be what sociologists study.* And the athe-

---

[4] For that matter, where does Jiminy Cricket come from? To answer, "from Walt Disney," is to say nothing. Most things come from Walt Disney. We must still ask: What makes Jiminy Cricket so smart? Granted, it is a noteworthy thing for a cricket to speak. But mynah birds and parrots can speak, too, and we don't let them dictate moral imperatives except for those few extraordinary circumstances in which we do.[5]

[5] I may, admittedly, be speaking here mainly for myself. Some years ago, while attending a party at the home of a university colleague, I found myself in the man's study. The rest of the guests were noisily congregating in the living room and the kitchen; I was quite alone. As one does, I was idly surveying the bookshelves, noting with varying degrees of approval, disappointment, or condemnation the presence of this title or that, or the absence of my own volume (*You Would Even Say It Glows: Evidence of Bioluminescence on Tundra, the Reindeer, as Observed at the San Diego Zoo.* Euphonia College Press, 2003). Then my eye fell upon a handsome decanter resting on a

ists believe (God knows how) that a bunch of people just got out of bed one day and said, "Hey! Since there's no God, let's invent morality!"

Of course, none of these "experts" can explain *why* we have morality. And when you pose that question to them, the best they can do is throw up their hands and say, "Science isn't allowed to talk about why." And when you reply, "Okay, but guess what. You're not real scientists," they say, "Yes we are, we're *social* scientists," and then they run away like a lot of pathetic cowards.

---

custom-made mahogany stand. A brass tag hanging by a fine chain around the bottle identified the contents as a particularly rare, expensive, and quite wonderful brandy. As there were two clean glasses on either side of the thing, I took the liberty of taking up one and pouring a modest two fingers' worth of the fragrant amber liquid. After all, I reasoned, I was a guest in the man's home, and he would want me to be entirely at ease. I had no sooner put the tumbler to my lips than I heard a harsh, squawking voice cry out, "He's taking the good stuff! He's taking the good stuff!" I staggered back, wheeled wildly, and only then saw the gray bird—parrotlike in shape, with a dash of crimson on its tail—in its vast cage in a corner of the room. Chuckling with amusement, I shook my head, toasted the creature with the glass, and again made to sip the elixir therein. "Better put it down! Put it down! He's taking the good stuff!" "My God, what is that noise?" a voice said in the hallway. "Robert's African gray," someone answered. "Come on, I'll show you." Deciding that the bird's ethical rebuke perhaps had some merit after all, I put the glass down and rapidly strode from the room.

In fact, there is only one explanation for the existence of morality in human affairs that makes sense, that explains what needs to be explained, and that accounts for the development of such noble (and distinctly human) qualities as selflessness, altruism, being polite, not hitting your sister, listening to your mother, and behaving yourself on a first date unless you receive certain signals.

Morality comes from Santa Claus.

This at first might seem surprising. Didn't morality exist before Santa Claus was born?[6] No, in fact it did not. Rather, up until that time, proper behavior in human society was largely the result of coercion and the fear of various kinds of reprimand, including stoning, heavy fines, torture, or public ridicule. One did not behave morally. Instead, one obeyed the law and—grudgingly, to be sure—curbed one's most antisocial impulses. Rather than murdering people with whom one disagreed, one simply beat them up. Rather than horsewhipping a man when he sneezed, one said, "Gesundheit."

---

[6] I find the idea that Santa Claus was born to be very disturbing. It seems deeply wrong and even faintly obscene. And yet how else could he have arrived on earth? I suppose he must have been born, but I don't like to think about it. The fact that some woman, somewhere, was the mother of Santa Claus is even worse.

It is only with the birth of Santa Claus that mankind's behavior begins to be shaped not by the threat of punishment but by a desire to get Christmas presents. (I realize I just shifted from the past tense in the previous paragraph to the present tense in this one, but I think that the use of the present tense when talking about events in the past makes everything more exciting.) Only then do the terms *naughty* and *nice* enter various cultures' basic vocabulary.

But this, the birth of morality itself, is only made possible by one essential fact: *Santa Claus has standards.*

While rightly famous for his role as The Supremo Presenter of Presents, Santa should not be mistaken for some mindlessly generous benefactor who bestows gifts on just anyone and everyone. Claus is many things, but he is no pushover. Indeed, we would not want him to be one. If he were—if he just gave us whatever we wanted, plus the batteries that are otherwise never included, the special ergonomic headphones, and the USB-ready dough hooks—his gift would have practically no value to us. We simply wouldn't care. We'd say, "Oh, really? For us? Oh, gee, thanks, Santa. No, really, it's perfect. We love it."

Instead, of course, every gift from Santa has about it a certain aura of prestige and importance precisely because he applies a famously rigorous set of standards to the matter of who gets what. When we receive something from Santa for Christmas, we don't just sneer to our family, friends, and colleagues in a sullen manner, "Guess what the fat man gave me *this* year." Instead, we beam with pride and, with a touch of delightful coyness, we say, "Guess what Santa gave me!" (I say "we" because this is how I react on Christmas day, and while there are aspects of my personality I consider absolutely unique, I cannot but assume my experience on that magical morning to be anything but universal.)

Why do we receive Santa's gifts with such a thrill of acceptance and validation? Because Santa is more than just the Bringer of Things We Want. He is the Bestower of Moral Approval. Santa Claus is nothing less than the moral arbiter of all those who participate in Christmas, and his judgments about our moral fitness determine whether we receive gifts equal in splendor to our very dreams or yet another Bun and Thigh Roller.

This is an even more magnificent and significant fact about Santa than those connected with his gift giving. To be sure, it is impressive to fly around the world in a single day and night, delivering gifts to millions of homes by hand. But once you have the equipment, personnel, and technology, almost any fat Christian male could do it who fit the most reasonable of criteria: (a) You must not be afraid to fly. (b) You must not be lactose or Oreo-intolerant. (c) You must not be allergic to reindeer. (d) You must be able, under heavy deadline pressure, to work with elves.

But if anyone, given a big enough sack and enough wrapping paper, can deliver presents to the world, not just anyone can, while doing it, consider the degree of moral fitness of each potential recipient. And yet Santa does this, year after year—and we respond to it. We are told to "be good" so that "Santa will bring us something." And we *are* good. And he *does* bring us something.

But another question now arises: How do we know all this? How do we know that Santa expects us to be good, which in turn causes us to be good, and so introduces the moral sense into human society?

We know because we are the recipients of a special creation that has endured for generations, in which every aspect of Santa's moral task is laid out for all to see. This work has been part of Western culture since before we were born, and its persistence to this day, its continuing relevance even to our modern, high-tech, cyberiffic a-go-go lives, attests to its profound influence on the human soul.

This work is called many things by many people, but its formal name is "Santa Claus Is Coming to Town." It was written—if *written* is the correct term for something so inspired—in 1932 by Haven Gillespie and J. Fred Coots. A close reading of the lyrics reveals many startling and important facts about Santa.

We begin with a portentous warning:

You better watch out!
You better not cry!
You better not pout!
I'm telling you why.
Santa Claus is comin' to town.

Santa, like some cross between a circuit-riding Judge Roy Bean and the bad guys from *High Noon*, is en route, and we had better prepare for his arrival. Tears, surliness, or any sort of defiant or negative grouchy attitude will avail nothing. We have been put on notice. Note that he "is comin' to town," which means that he doesn't live here, in town. He lives elsewhere and is coming here. The implication is obvious: he has been to other towns. And yet no specific town is mentioned, leaving us to conclude that he is comin' to all towns at the same time. Thus, the first of Santa's transcendent characteristics is established: He is omnipresent, or at least he will be, once he comes to town.

It is important that we know all this, considering what follows:

He's making a list
And checking it twice.
He's gonna find out
Who's naughty and nice.
Santa Claus is comin' to town.

Here, in the plainest of words, is the explicit equivalence between Santa and the God of the Old Testament, Jehovah-Yahweh, Lord of the Jews who, every Yom Kippur, evaluates His people's previous year's actions for good or ill, notes their degree of repentance and atonement, and then writes—or doesn't write—their name in the Book of Life. Also invoked is St. Peter, guardian of the Gate of Heaven, who consults a big book (his own list) to see if the souls of the newly dead are worthy of admission to Paradise.

"But what if Santa makes a mistake?" is the common cry of the aggrieved or the fearful or the underinsured. "What if I've been nice, but he writes me down as having been naughty?" He makes no mistakes. He makes a list, and then checks it twice, i.e., he notes one's naughtiness or niceness no fewer than three times. Three times! What else do you want?![7]

But Santa's role as moral judge rests on more than mere thoroughness. Behold:

> *He sees you when you're sleeping.*
> *He knows when you're awake.*

---

7 Again, I make use of the ?! mark. I must confess I am tempted to employ it on a regular basis and thus feature it as a trademark of my writing style. Should I?! I think so. Don't you?! *[No!—Ed.]*

He knows if you've been bad or good.
So be good for goodness' sake!

How, our scientist friends like to ask, is this possible? Does Santa, like Superman, have X-ray vision? Does he plant covert surveillance devices in our bedrooms when he visits? Oh, I know! Santa Claus works for the CIA! Ha-ha-ha!

No, it is most assuredly not funny. The truth, of course, is much simpler: Santa is omniscient.

Indeed, he would have to be. How else would he be able to discern any given individual's naughtiness or niceness? By asking? Please. Which of us would willingly confess our naughtiness to Santa himself?

No, his very ability to *be* Santa Claus depends on his being omniscient. "He *knows* if you've been bad or good." (Italics added.) How does he know? Not because he's told, or he spies, or he asks, or he deploys monitoring technology; not because he distributes questionnaires or bribes family members to report on each other. And while it is true that his surrogates go through the charade of questioning whatever children appear before them ("Have you been a good boy this year?"), even the children themselves, one feels, sense the empty formality of this ritual. You may depend on it that each of them, from the most blameless little angel to the monster newly exhausted from disemboweling his grandmother with a paring knife, answers "Yes."

But Santa knows the truth. He knows because he's Santa Claus.

Thus the warning acquires additional force when repeated:

> *So you better watch out!*
> *You better not cry!*
> *You better not pout!*
> *I'm telling you why.*
> *Santa Claus is comin' to town.*

These stanzas, thus far, comprise the part of the song with which everyone is familiar. But scholars have pointed out that there is an additional bridge to the song that usually goes ignored:

> *The kids in girl and boyland*
> *Will have a jubilee.*
> *They're gonna build a toyland town,*
> *All around the Christmas tree.*

At first we wonder: Why is this perfectly cute verse so often omitted? True, there is no actual place called "girl and boyland," unless it is the land where the girls and boys live who sit in the laps of those who live in Lapland. But I have never seen this theory confirmed.

Nonetheless, let us suppose that "girl and boyland" is not a real place. So what? (Or, rather, so what?![8]) In a song as important and sacred as this, the use of an imaginary place name merely contributes to the mythic, timeless spirit of its magical and fantastical kind of wondrous delightfulness that is as beautiful as it is lovely.

But a second reading reveals the problem: What business do any of the kids in girl and boyland have making plans for a jubilee, *when Santa Claus has not yet come to town?* Which among them dares to presume that he or she will be deemed nice? The entire thrust of the first verse is thus obviated and nullified. There is nothing to watch out for and no reason not to pout.

No wonder this stanza is hardly ever sung. No wonder it has failed to follow the verses and the first bridge into the canon of accepted sacred Christmas/Clausian liturgy. It makes a mockery of Santa's role as the Great Judge of Merit and, like a verse of the Bible that con-

---

[8] Ibid. or op. cit., or whatever the appropriate abbreviation is. I'm sure my editor will know. [*I do know the appropriate abbreviation, but I'm so irritated by the tone of these endnotes that I'm not going to tell you.—Ed.*] Of course, whether or not he will bother to correct it is entirely another matter. [*Oh, be quiet and move on.—Ed.*][9]

[9] They are, of course, not endnotes. They're footnotes.

tradicts accepted doctrine, may and indeed must be ignored.

The song ends with its original caveat, and a promise of Clausian return:

> *So you better watch out!*
> *You better not cry!*
> *You better not pout!*
> *I'm telling you why.*
> *Santa Claus is comin' to town.*

An announcement of impending judgment, a threat of possible punishment, a promise of virtue rewarded. Would any of this possess such power and influence over millions of our fellow human beings if it concerned a person who did not exist? From where else could we have derived our most fundamental intuitions about what it means to be truly naughty, if not from the great Arbiter of Naughtiness himself?

Let us put it plainly: because of how we feel about him, and because of how he makes us feel about ourselves, Santa Claus must surely exist.

Santa flees a naughty boy—possibly an unbeliever-in-Santa—out to "get" him. Note confederate lurking at roof entrance. Attacks on Santa's person have increased dramatically over the past thirty years—additional proof that he exists.

A Final Word

OBVIOUSLY, Santa Claus exists.

I say this not because, like a clergyman, my entire life and career and livelihood and self-image depend upon the existence of a being whom millions claim is a fiction but because I have demonstrated it beyond any reasonable doubt. Now it is up to each of us to put that knowledge into action, to live our lives, not as if Santa existed but because he *does* exist.

Because he does. You've read the book, and you know that he just does.

Given that magnificent fact, we must then ask: How should we live? And, more important, how shall we deal with those who still don't believe Santa exists? Someone will say, "Just leave them alone. It's a free country. Live and let live." But why? What if their denial of Santa's existence hurts his feelings? What if it hurts *our* feelings?

Indifference (or outright hostility) to the existence of Santa Claus may be perfectly acceptable in other cultures. But we are a Christmas-celebrating nation. Our Founding Fathers (with the exception of Benjamin Franklin, who was probably Jewish) gave each other secret Santa gifts and sang carols at the Continental Congress's annual Christmas party. Thomas Jefferson invented the candy cane.

There is something un-American and therefore terrible about not believing in Santa Claus. That is why it is incumbent on all of us to show the skeptics the error of their ways, to encourage and to enable them to believe. And, while heretofore that task was almost insurmountable, we now have in our arsenal a very special tool to make the job infinitely easier.

I refer to this book.

If every reader of this work were to purchase two additional copies and give them to a pair of Santa-denying relatives, friends, or colleagues, and if they, in turn, were to do the same, I feel in my heart that we might very well see the cultural, religious, and moral landscape of the great nation of this country change literally before our eyes from a land of discord to a place of harmony, from a troubled city in a valley of contention to a shining mall on a hill, from a divided society of the Naughty and the Nice to a unified and worthy people— one Nation, under Claus, with presents and special treats for all.

March 2005
Los Angeles, California

APPENDIX

Lesser Arguments

A. Pascal's Wager

B. The Argument from Fame

C. The Argument from Truism

PASCAL'S WAGER

One of the most famous arguments in the history of the philosophy of religion is Pascal's Wager, named for the French philosopher and mathematician Blaise Pascal (1623–1662). The wager, included in Pascal's seminal work *Pensées* (*Thoughts*), holds that it is rational to believe in God (to bet on God's existence) on the basis of a comparison of the different outcomes one will face after death, depending on whether God exists or not. If God exists, and you have chosen to believe in Him, you gain eternal bliss; if He exists and you have elected not to believe, you face eternal torment in hell. If, after you die, it turns out that God does not exist, you have lost nothing either way. Thus put, it is in one's best interest and it makes rational sense to believe in God, just in case He does exist.

There is a mountain of commentary both in support of and in refutation of this argument, but fortunately we may ignore both, since this is not the Pascal's Wager to which I refer. The sad fact is that Blaise Pascal had absolutely nothing to say about the existence of Santa Claus. Either he didn't believe in Santa, or had never heard of him, or just didn't have any santalogical *pensées* worth recording.

No, the Pascal's Wager I refer to has been proposed by Barry Pascal, a member of a Usenet group to which I belong, one with the inelegant name alt.rec.phil.claus. WhoIs?.santa.proof.OhYeah?.Yeah.Debate.ShutUp.You ShutUp.org.net. The substance of Barry Pascal's argument goes something like this:

Santa exists whether I believe in him or not, so I should believe in him. If I don't, then I'm an idiot. If I do believe in him, then people who don't believe in him are idiots but I am not.

We may present the argument in graphical form in the following table, also created by me in Microsoft Word:

RESULT MATRIX OF PASCAL'S WAGER

	Santa Claus Exists	Santa Claus Does Not Exist
I do not believe in Santa Claus	I am an idiot.	Yes he does, so I am an idiot.
I believe in Santa Claus	I am not an idiot.	Yes he does, so *you* are an idiot

There are certain things that must be said about this argument. They include:

1. It is not nice to call people idiots.

2. Therefore, it is naughty to call people idiots.

3. It is stipulated that Santa will not bring you presents if you are naughty.

4. It is rational and reasonable to want Santa to bring you presents.

5. Therefore, this argument, however valid its claim on truth, should not be used except in private, when speaking among people who already agree

with you, while you are all complaining about how modern secular society is so horrible and oppressive in its persecution of believers in Claus. By restricting your discussion of this matter to fellow believers, you avoid any temptation or obligation to call someone an idiot, thus incurring the disapproval of you-know-who.

I refer to this argument as Pascal's Wager because Barry Pascal bet me ten dollars I "wouldn't have the guts" to include it in this book. That I do have the guts and that I have won the wager are self-evident and irrefutable. Pascal will thus have to pay ten dollars to learn something about my intellectual integrity, but it is a lesson he will not soon forget.

THE ARGUMENT FROM FAME

Everybody knows who Santa Claus is. And while fame in and of itself is no guarantor of existence, sooner or later the reasonable person has to ask him- or herself, "How can this person, so beloved and well-known, so instantly recognizable in photographs and in person, so universally referred to as being synonymous with generosity, so emblematic of not only a world-famous holiday of one of the world's great religions but, indeed, of an entire season—how can this person not exist?"

That's all I'm saying. You just have to wonder. Don't you? I know I do.

THE ARGUMENT FROM TRUISM

The argument from truism, first advanced by me about fifteen minutes ago when I made it up, rests upon a premise of admittedly controversial ontological validity, but then quickly reaches the desired conclusion. Here it is:

It is universally agreed that you're nobody 'til somebody loves you. Everybody loves Santa Claus. Therefore, he is somebody. Since it is impossible to be somebody without existing, Santa Claus must exist.

Granted, at first blush this seems a slightly more sophisticated, hip, Dean Martinesque version of the ontological argument. Like St. Anselm's proof, mine begins with a definition, then moves with supple, languid ease to its inevitable conclusion. However, it does raise certain issues that deserve to be considered:

a. Once somebody loves you, do you remain somebody? Or are you only somebody once somebody *begins to* love you, after which you resume being nobody?

b. The somebody who loves you can only *be* somebody if somebody loves him or her. If no one does, then by definition that person is really nobody. Thus, the strictest formulation of the premise of the argument from truism would be: You're nobody 'til nobody loves you, at which point you become somebody. If you love them back, or if some other third party loves them during this time, then they, too, become somebody.

c. Was there ever a time in which Santa Claus was nobody? Or has he always been subject a priori to being loved?

These and similar questions are more suited to professional debate and therefore exceed the limits of the present inquiry, particularly in light of the paltry advance I have received for said work.

Ellis Weiner has been an editor at *National Lampoon*, a columnist for *Spy*, and is the author of *Drop Dead, My Lovely* and *The Big Boat to Bye-Bye*. He is co-author of *Yiddish with Dick and Jane*. He lives in California. His website is a mess.